I LIKE TO READ

Written by
Brian and Anne Moses

Illustrated by
Sharon Davey

CRABTREE
PUBLISHING COMPANY
WWW.CRABTREEBOOKS.COM

First published in Great Britain in 2022 by The Watts
Publishing Group
Copyright © The Watts Publishing Group, 2022
First published in Great Britain in 2022 by The Watts
Publishing Group
Copyright © The Watts Publishing Group, 2022

Author: Brian and Anne Moses
Series Editor: Melanie Palmer
Series Design: Lisa Peacock
Literacy Consultant: Kate Ruttle
Editorial director: Kathy Middleton
Illustrator: Sharon Davey
Editor: Janine Deschenes
Proofreader: Petrice Custance
Production technician: Margaret Salter
Print coordinator: Katherine Berti

Library and Archives Canada Cataloguing in Publication

CIP Available at the Library and Archives Canada

Library of Congress Cataloging-in-Publication Data

CIP Available at the Library of Congress

Crabtree Publishing Company
www.crabtreebooks.com   1-800-387-7650

Published by Crabtree Publishing Company in 2022.

Printed in the U.S.A./012022/CG20210915

Published in Canada
Crabtree Publishing
616 Welland Ave.
St. Catharines, Ontario
L2M 5V6

Published in the United States
Crabtree Publishing
347 Fifth Ave
Suite 1402-145
New York, NY 10016

I LIKE TO READ

Written by
Brian and Anne Moses

Illustrated by
Sharon Davey

CRABTREE
PUBLISHING COMPANY
WWW.CRABTREEBOOKS.COM

Hannah, Wang Li, Levi, and William are learning to read.

Willliam likes to visit the bookstore near his house. Sometimes he picks out a lot of books!

Wang Li loves to go to the library. She finds a quiet corner to read with her brother.

Each day at bedtime, Wang Li asks to read her favorite story.

Do you really want to read this one again?

They take turns to read each page of the story.

Everyone has a favorite place to read.

When the weather is warm and the bees are buzzing, Levi and William like to read in Levi's backyard.

Hannah likes to settle down in the shade of the sunflowers in her yard.

Every summer, Wang Li
and her family fly to China
to visit her grandparents.

It is a long plane ride! Wang Li brings several books to read. She brings some reading games, too. Her favorite game is reading bingo!

William enjoys reading facts about dinosaurs. He likes to picture how they looked and sounded.

Hannah likes to read poetry. She loves to read her favorite poems to the children in her class. Today, she has chosen a poem about a dragon.

Meet Lucy, the Labrador retriever.
All the children love reading to Lucy
when she comes into school.

Reading to Lucy is great practice! Lucy helps the children feel comfortable too.

Hannah and Wang Li are reading about the oceans. Today, they are finding information about ocean pollution. They learned that there is a lot of plastic in the oceans.

They are going to find more information on the Internet. They want to read about ways they can help.

On the weekend, Hannah visits a zoo with her family. She is reading an information screen that shows her useful facts about elephants.

William helps his dad make a pizza. They read the recipe carefully. It will taste delicious!

23

It's a lot of fun when the children celebrate Book Day at school.

It is a day when each student shares their favorite book with their classmates. They also dress up as their favorite book characters!

Sometimes, a story gets so exciting that William doesn't want to stop reading. He can't wait to tell his family all about the story.

Our teacher says it is important to read so we can stretch our imaginations.

She says that reading is a ticket to an adventure.

28

NOTES FOR CAREGIVERS AND EDUCATORS

From inspiring creativity to cultivating learning, this book shows that reading is both important and fun. Children will be inspired to take an interest in improving their reading skills and sharing books with their family and peers. Here are some ideas for how to get the most from this book.

Pages 4–5 and 6–7
Make a list of reasons why reading is important. Talk about all the places at home, at school, and in the community where reading is needed. Why might reading be important at the grocery store, for example? How about while going for a walk in their neighborhoods?

Pages 8–9
Visit your local library. Let children choose books to borrow. Make visiting the library a regular activity. Talk about the books they borrow and why they made those particular choices.

Pages 10–11
Ask children to share their favorite books. What do they like about them? Talk to children about the books that you like to read, too. What was your favorite book as a child? Share it with children, if available.

Pages 12–13
Where do children like to read? Why do they choose these places? Encourage them to use adjectives to describe their reading places. If possible, create a reading spot at home or in the classroom, with children's input.

Pages 14-15

Wang Li loves to play reading games while she is on the plane. Her favorite is reading bingo. Create your own reading bingo game. It can include short-term goals, such as finding words and sounds within one book, or long-term goals, such as reading books of different genres and with different lengths. Try out some other reading games too, such as concentration and rhyming challenges.

Page 16-17

Enjoy reading poetry with children. If it's a rhyming poem, pick out the words that rhyme. Explore reading different kinds of poetry, such as shape poems, haiku, and limericks.

Page 18-19

Reading to others is a great way to practice reading skills and feel comfortable. Encourage children to read to each other, to their pets, and even to a group of stuffed animals!

Pages 20-21 and 22-23

Use the Internet to find facts about a topic that interests children. Design a sign or poster that tells others the most important facts.

Pages 24-25

Ask children which book character they would dress up as. Ask them to design a costume. Can they think of a new character that could appear in their favorite book?

Pages 26-27 and 28-29

Read a new book together with children. Pick out new words to say aloud and discover their meaning. Stop after some pages and ask children to predict what might happen next. Ask children questions about the book when finished reading to improve their comprehension.

BOOKS TO SHARE

Again
by Emily Gravett (Simon & Schuster, 2013)

Charlie Cook's Favorite Book
by Julia Donaldson, illustrated by Axel Scheffler (Puffin Books, 2008)

Luna Loves Library Day
by Joseph Coelho and Fiona Lumbers (Anderson Press, 2018)

Walking With My Iguana
by Brian Moses, illustrated by Ed Boxall (Troika Books, 2020)

I Read-n-Rhyme series

by Craig Lopetz, Sebastian Smith,
and Taylor Farley (Crabtree Publishing, 2021)